The Leeds Mission, Commencing Jan. 24th, 1875: Its Objects, History and Results

May 31. 1875.

THE VICARAGE,

LEEDS.

Sir

In compliance with a
request from Mr Ingram I
sent you on Saturday a
Report of the Leeds mission.

It was drawn up hastily
in Passion week by one of our
Secretaries, and therefore is
not as complete or concise
as it should have been.

The results are naturally difficult to give. But I can say that it has ^united the clergy of the town into a compact body, it carried the Dissenters almost in a mass on its tide, it increased our Congregations & Schools, it doubled the following annual Confirmations, it has led to the formation of a House of Mercy. |

I can lay my hand upon many fallen women who are reclaimed by it, very many persons of respe...

& deepened the religion of the best,
converted hearts, many
new religious classes have
had & be formed for various
kinds of persons, & the number
of those doing church work
has been largely increased.

⌐ Though every clergyman
was left free to work as he
chose, yet the town became
like one Parish, the shops
closed early, the mills &
foundaries all, or very nearly
all, gave their time, prepared
the conveniences needful for a
congregation, & at their own cost

had missionary services either from the Bishop of the Diocese or the clergy.

The results are still going on, & new fruits of the mission are constantly appearing.

The great want it has left is the cry for more clergy to occupy the new ground, and I spent last week in Oxford to obtain men, and I go to the Theological Colleges in the South this week and next for the same purpose

I am, Sir
yours faithfully
H. Wilberforce
Vicar, Oxford

THE LEEDS MISSION.

THE LEEDS MISSION for which long and anxious preparation
was made, to which many looked forward with hope and some
with misgiving, from which blessings were expected from the
Great Head of the Church in answer to united and earnest
prayer, is now a thing of the past—the Leeds Mission has
come and gone.

The objects for which the Mission was undertaken have
been more than realised, the most sanguine anticipations more
than fulfilled. Whilst, knowing God's willingness to hear and
answer the prayers of His people, His promises, which have
never been withdrawn, to further the efforts of those who
humbly and earnestly endeavour to advance the Kingdom of
Christ, knowing too how Special Missions in other places have
been the means under God of awakening careless sinners,
arousing those at ease in Zion, reclaiming backsliders, and
stirring up Christians generally to greater diligence, greater
earnestness, greater love to the Saviour, greater desires after personal holiness, greater longings and endeavours "to follow the
example of our Saviour Christ and to be made like unto Him,"
whilst from all these considerations we had sufficient reason
to look for the aid and blessing of the Holy Spirit in carrying
out the Mission—few, if any, dared to hope for so large an
outpouring of the Spirit as He has been pleased to vouchsafe.

It was indeed well said towards the close of the Mission
Week, by one of the clergymen conducting the mid-day
devotional service in the Church Institute, "The effects of the
Leeds Mission have been and are truly wonderful. Thousands

B

are flocking to hear the Word of God, the inquiry is heard on every side, 'What must I do to be saved?' the whole town seems shaken by the Spirit of God. Pentecostal showers of blessings are falling: as in the earliest days of the Christian Church the Lord worked with His servants and confirmed the Word with signs following, so it is now. And yet, perhaps, we ought not to call the work now progressing wonderful : is it not the very thing we have long been praying for, the very thing we have been aiming at, hoping for, looking for? is it not just what God has promised to grant when the prayer of faith is offered and true and real effort put forth in the way He has commanded? Believing in God's promises, having experienced and witnessed the power of His Spirit, we ought not to be surprised at the evident tokens of His love and favour which He is manifesting at this time."

It has been thought desirable that an account of the Mission should be printed—

1. Because many of the clergy and church workers of the town, occupied as they were during the Mission in their own parishes, desire to know how the Lord's work progressed in other parts of Leeds.

As in a battle the soldier sees little beyond that portion of the field in which he is himself engaged, so in a Mission ; and those who took an active though ever so humble a part in the attack upon the vice and godlessness prevalent in their own district, naturally wish to learn something of what was done where they could not be eye-witnesses.

2. Because many—particularly those who received special blessings to their own souls during the Mission, either by being brought for the first time to see Jesus as their Saviour, and to accept the invitation of the Gospel, or by being stimulated to more earnestness in 'Christian life and work—expressed the wish to have some permanent record of that which had, by the blessing of God, brought such a transforming, quickening, gladdening change upon their hearts and lives. Such a record would be to them a perpetual remembrance of past mercies,

and a reminder of His promises of present and future help and guidance As they looked on such a record they would realise something of David's feeling when he said, "The Lord *hath been* mindful of us, and He *will bless us.*"

3 Inasmuch as Special Missions are becoming more and more a recognised form of Church work throughout the land, it was felt that any account of a Mission so signally owned of God as was this in Leeds, would be read with interest, and it was hoped with spiritual profit, not only by many interested in the true welfare of their fellow men by the extension of Christ's Kingdom, but especially by any in other towns or districts who might desire to have a mission in their own neighbourhood. The experience of one often serves as a guide to many (It may be added, that for a like reason, a portfolio, containing specimens of all the General, and of nearly all the Parochial Papers circulated during the Mission, has been placed for reference in the Church Institute Library.)

All who have had any practical acquaintance with the subject agree that a Special Mission is not a thing to be taken up lightly, or without previous and long preparation. "In all labour there is profit," and certainly spiritual labour is no exception God owns and abundantly blesses the diligent use of means placed within man's reach.

The Leeds Mission was not undertaken or commenced hastily, as will be seen from the fact, that at a Meeting of the Ruri-Decanal Chapter, held April 13, 1874, it was resolved that a Special Meeting of the Clergy should be held on April 17th, to which the Rev. G H. Wilkinson, Vicar of St. Peter's, Eaton Square, well known throughout the land as a Missioner whose labours were remarkably successful, should be invited. He attended, and gave counsel as to the best way of conducting a Mission.

Many valuable suggestions, which proved most useful afterwards, were given respecting the various ways in which Church workers could help forward a Mission, respecting the mode of conducting services, after meetings, &c.

At a subsequent Meeting of the Chapter, held April 28, the Rev. W. H. M. H. Aitken, of Christ Church, Everton, Liverpool, also widely known 'for his special gifts as a Mission Preacher, and for his great .experience in Mission work, addressed the clergy. He gave many hints, subsequently acted upon, as to organisation, handbills that should be circulated, plans by which the Gospel might be taken to the various districts of the town, &c.

It was then unanimously resolved to hold a Mission. The note of preparation was thus struck nine or ten months before the event itself took place. It will appear in the narrative how that comparatively long period was employed.

A Committee of the Clergy was appointed fairly representative of the different localities, &c., to make arrangements for the Mission. It consisted of the following:—

The Rev. Dr. GOTT, Vicar of Leeds, Rural Dean, *Chairman*.
Rev. S. ADAMS, Vicar of St. George's.
Rev. R. DOUGLAS, Rector of Farnley.
Rev. Dr. FLOOD, Vicar of St. Matthew's.
Rev. J. H. GOODIER, Vicar of St. Jude's, Hunslet.
Rev. J. HEPHER, Vicar of St. John's, Newtown.
Rev. E. JACKSON, Incumbent of St. James's.
Rev. A. H. KELK, Vicar of Burmantofts.
Rev. R. R. KIRBY, Vicar of Chapeltown.
Rev. J. H. McCHEANE, Incumbent of Holy Trinity.
Rev. H. TEMPLE, Vicar of St. John's.
Rev. J. MAUGHAN, Vicar of Armley Hall.
Rev. F. J. WOOD, Clerk-in-Orders, Parish Church.
Rev. F. G. HUME SMITH, Incumbent of Armley, } *Hon.*
Rev. THOS. WHITBY, Vicar of St. Simon's, } *Secretaries.*
   THOS. HARRISON, Esq., Wyther, *Treasurer*.

The Bishop of Ripon from the beginning shewed the deepest interest in the Mission. He promised to write a Pastoral Letter, addressed to the people of Leeds, on the subject; and, as will be seen hereafter, took a most active part in conducting the work itself.

A circular was sent to all the Clergy of the Rural Deanery, asking them to tell the people of their parishes of the forthcoming Mission, and to ask their prayers in private and in

their families for its success.   It was arranged that simulta-
neous sermons on the subject should be preached throughout
Leeds on Sunday, June 28th.

Monday, Sept 28th, was set apart as one of Special Preparation on the part of the Clergy

At 10 a m. on that day the Clergy assembled at the Parish
Church for Morning Prayer

At 11 a.m there was the Administration of the Holy Communion and a Sermon by the Bishop of Ripon, from 2 Chron.
xxix 36: "And Hezekiah rejoiced, and all the people, that
God had prepared the people." His Lordship, after expressing
his gladness that a Mission was to take place, and his pleasure
at being invited to address his reverend brethren on a subject
of such importance and interest, said: "I will speak to you
with regard to—

"1st, The Objects of the Mission; 2ndly, The Means to be
employed to secure its Success, and 3rdly, The Results which
we may reasonably anticipate from the Mission.

"I. The minister's work is partly pastoral, partly missionary;
pastoral as regards his congregation, missionary to those outside who seldom or never come to the house of God, and who
are careless as to their eternal interests.   One great object of
the Mission is to bring the Gospel message to every home and
every heart, so that none in the several parishes may be able
to say in the Great Day of account, 'No man cared for my
soul'"   Another object of the Mission is to leave the beaten
track, and by a special effort to endeavour to arouse the members of our congregations who are but Christians in name, to
rebuke their lethargy, to raise them to a higher spiritual
level.

"II. There can be no success to the Mission unless God the
Holy Ghost gives spiritual life In dependence on His promised
aid we must—

(1) "Recognise the magnitude of the work to be done.
     A combined attack is to be made on the empire of
     Satan.

(2) "Examine well the state of our own hearts. We who
     are Christian ministers need greater zeal, humility,
     love ; more of the mind of Christ.

(3) "Not only amongst the clergy, but amongst the people
     at large there must be preparation for the Mission.
     Sunday school teachers, district visitors, tract dis-
     tributors, Church workers, should pray for its success,
     speak of it to others; and, when January comes, take
     part in it.

(4) " In the Mission, and in preparation for it, Christ and
     Christ alone must be exalted.   Let there be no
     divisions, no party feeling, no aim lower than this—
     to exalt the Redeemer and to bring souls to Christ.

" III. If God gives success, as I trust He will, we may
anticipate—

(1) " A higher standard of spirituality amongst ourselves.

(2) " Greater union.

(3) " The conversion of souls.

(4) " Larger congregations and growth in zeal and holiness.

(5) " An increase in the number of persons who openly pro-
     fess Christian discipleship by presenting themselves
     for Confirmation.

(6) " An increase in the number of Communicants.

" These are great results.   They have accompanied and
followed Special Missions in other towns, and I trust they will
do so in Leeds."

In the course of the afternoon, addresses were given by the
Rev. F. Pigou, Vicar of Doncaster, and the Rev. Canon Furse,
Principal of Cuddesdon College.

Mr. Pigou said that, " In the Mission the Cross of Christ
must be lifted up, and men will assuredly be drawn to it.
Opposition must be expected, and even welcomed, as a sign of
real work being done for God.   All undue excitement must be

avoided. It is found that the results of a Mission are most enduring where there has been the least excitement. Much may be hoped for, nothing need be feared, from a Mission."

Canon Furse said that, "We could not tell to what class the Mission would prove most useful. Sometimes the greatest effects of a Mission are seen not so much in those who are unconverted, as in advancing and deepening the religious life of those already converted. A Mission is not meant as an occasion for pressing our own views on others, or even for strengthening the Established Church, but simply to act on individual souls, and win them to Christ"

Early in October about 60,000 copies of the Pastoral Address of the Bishop of Ripon to the People of Leeds were circulated throughout the town and read in nearly all the Churches The Bishop spoke in the Pastoral of the need of a Mission. "Tens of thousands are living without God in the world. Multitudes around us, with souls to be everlastingly saved or lost, are passing through life in the busy pursuit of gain or pleasure, but in the utter neglect of God, of Eternity of Heaven; of Hell. Many have been ensnared by the artifices of the infidel and the scoffer A large proportion attend no place of public worship The Sabbath and Sabbath Ordinances they altogether disregard Some of our Churches are only half filled. Drunkenness, profane swearing, vice, irreligion, and crime are found in our midst. Many, it is to be feared, who make a profession of religious belief, live far below the standard which their profession demands. These are acknowledged crying evils . . Special Missions have been tried elsewhere with a marked result for good. Why should not a blessing follow from such a Mission in Leeds? I heartily commend this Special Mission to the sympathy and the prayers of all faithful disciples of Christ, who desire that the kingdom of Satan may be weakened and the kingdom of Christ may be strengthened."

Devotional meetings of the clergy were held fortnightly in the Antechapel of the Parish Church, and, as the Mission approached, weekly. These meetings lasted an hour, and were conducted by three clergymen, each of whom read a portion of Scripture (with or without short exposition), and prayed, (either extempore or otherwise). Besides these more general gatherings, smaller companies of the clergy, members of various clerical societies, assembled to ask God's blessing on the Mission. Parochial councils, cottage lectures, school meetings for prayer, for practising hymns and tunes, for arranging Christian work, were all set in motion with direct reference to the special effort about to be made.

A paper similar to one issued at the London Mission, containing hints and suggestions as to the mode of conducting a Mission, was sent to every clergyman in the town.

The Committee recommended that the Form of Service and Mission Hymn Book, published by the Society for Promoting Christian Knowledge, and sanctioned by the Bishop of Ripon, should be adopted, and most of the churches used those books. That great Society kindly made grants, varying in value from £2 to £10, of Tracts, Mission Hymn Books, and Services, to the poorer parishes of Leeds.

Having decided to hold during the Mission Week a Special Mission to Fallen Women, the Committee invited three London Clergymen, who had had large experience in such work, to confer with them, and much useful information was thus gained.

The Bishop of Ripon having expressed his intention to spend the Week in Leeds and to take part in the work of the Mission, it was decided to ask his Lordship to give addresses in the larger mills and workshops of the town, should the opportunities of doing so be afforded. The Bishop most cordially fell in with this request.

For weeks before the Mission large placards were posted throughout the borough, one of them simply, " Leeds Mission, will commence, God Willing, Sunday, Jan 24, 1875." Another contained the names of all the Churches taking part in the Mission A third, that appeared on notice boards, on the walls, on and in the tram cars, at Church doors, every-where, read thus :—

LEEDS
MISSION,
SUNDAY, JAN. 24TH,
AND THE FOLLOWING DAYS.

What is a Mission?

A Message from God to the Careless
and to all anxious about Eternity.

" I have an Errand to Thee."

" The Master is come and calleth for
Thee."

Think why He wants you.

Think why you want Him.

An important feature that marked the Mission from its very commencement, seen, indeed even in the preparation for it, was the interest it excited amongst all classes; the desire that it should be successful was felt by Churchmen and Nonconformists, the employers and employed, men of work and men of leisure. Leading articles and notices appeared in the local newspapers. Party going was largely suspended, arrangements that had been made for social and private gatherings to be held during the Mission time were set aside, tradesmen were requested by means of newspaper advertisements and bills on the walls to close their places of

business at 7 p.m. during the week, and bills for the shops
taken by the parochial clergy, appeared in the windows for
some days before January 24th, " During the Mission Week
this shop will be closed at 7 o'clock every evening except
Saturday."

Many publicans having expressed the wish that all public
houses might be closed on the two Sundays of the Mission,
letters were sent to the Committees of the Licensed Victuallers'
and of the Wine and Beersellers' Associations to ask for their
co-operation with the Mission Committee to effect this object.
The former replied, wishing the Mission every success, but
adding that however willing they might be to promote the
objects of the Mission, they had no legal power to act in the
matter.

The Secretary of the Wine and Beersellers' Association in his
answer said, " I beg to state that the Committee will use their
utmost endeavours to further your wishes on the two days
named, January 24th and 31st, and will give every opportunity
to their families and employés to attend the services of the
Mission."

Large employers of labour were applied to to allow the
Bishop to address their workpeople in the mills, and the
response was truly wonderful; indeed the Committee were
repeatedly obliged to decline applications made by masters of
mills, &c., for the Bishop to address the men.

It ought to be recorded, that wherever his Lordship addressed
the workpeople, the masters most willingly sacrificed their own
convenience and money too, inasmuch as the addresses were
given one and all in the masters' time. To stop machinery
and pay the wages for the half hour or three-quarters of an
hour that the services lasted in workshops, where, as was often
the case, between 1000 and 2000 men were employed, sometimes at a cost of £100 or £200, shewed no slight interest in
the Mission, and in the spiritual welfare of the workpeople.
In one instance the head of an important firm wrote to say
that if the Bishop would come, all the machinery throughout

the works should be stopped at any hour of the day or night. That no noise might disturb the service, a large room should be prepared; if in the evening, gas should be put in where needed, and bills, hymns, or any other papers provided at the expense of the firm; the letter ended by expressing the hope that the Bishop would remain at the works as long as he could.

Saturday, January 23rd, was set apart for solemn preparation and united prayer on the part of the clergy

This, the day before the commencement of the Mission, was selected to give an opportunity to the Mission preachers to take part in the services.

A large number of the clergy were present at the Parish Church, where, at 8 a m , there was the administration of the Holy Communion At 10, Morning Prayer, and an address by the Rev. G. H. Wilkinson, in the course of which he compared the work of the coming week with that set before the little band that issued from the upper room in Jerusalem If those who were to take part in the Leeds Mission would hope for such mighty results as were accomplished in early days, if they wished to see the whole of the borough laid low before the power of God, they must first believe that God the Father had reconciled the world unto Himself, that He had sent them with a message, and that they were not merely going to pass through certain religious ordinances, but were emphatically commissioned by God to take the message of the Father to the world. They went to the work of this Mission not as individuals but as one band, strengthened by the prayers of the whole fellowship of the faithful. In the strength of God the Mission could never end in failure, for God had said that all power was His, and that if they asked in the name of His Son their prayers would be answered, and the blessed Spirit's presence was covenanted unto them. Therefore, in the name of the Father, of the Son, and of the Holy Ghost, would they go forth to this enterprise.

At the close of the address, the Rev. Dr. Gott, Vicar of
Leeds, read the following letter from the Bishop of Edinburgh.

1, Athole Place, Edinburgh, January 20th, 1875

My DEAR SIR,—We have been holding during the past week in our
churches in this city a mission, which we trust and believe that it has pleased
God greatly to bless to the quickening of spiritual life amongst us. And as
we know that you are purposing to begin a mission in Leeds next Sunday, I
have undertaken to write to you in the name of my clergy, as well as on my
own behalf, to convey to you the expression of our sincere and deep sympathy
with you and with those who will engage with you in this blessed work, and
to assure you that you will be expressly remembered in our prayers during
your mission week.   Our attention has been called to your mission
from the fact that some of those whom we asked to help us had already
undertaken to assist you, and some of your papers have reached us   We
earnestly trust that the blessing which we have found may be very largely
poured out on you, and we trust also that you will remember us and our
Church in your prayers, so that the bonds of brotherly love, in the unity of
the same faith and the same Spirit, may be strengthened by the spiritual communion in our one Lord Jesus Christ.

Believe me, yours ever in Christ,
H COTTERILL, Bishop of Edinburgh.

Rev J Gott, Vicar of Leeds

Then followed intercessory prayer, the Vicar mentioning
various subjects, after intervals of a minute for silent intercession, on behalf of the particular object for which prayers were
desired. At noon there was the Litany, and one or two hymns
having been sung, the Rev. Prebendary Thynne gave a short
address, in the course of which he referred to some of the diffi-
culties connected with Mission work, and exhorted his hearers
not to be discouraged by apparent failures, pointing out that
success would not always be seen, and that many of the results
would only be known on the last Great Day. At half-past
one o'clock a conference of clergy was held in the Parochial
Room, and Missioners were appointed to give short addresses
and to conduct the devotions at the Church Institute,
Albion Place, from 2 15 to 3 p m. during the coming week—
two for each day.

There was a unanimous feeling that all Christians, whether
belonging to our own communion or not, should be invited to

pray for the success of the Mission, a large bill was therefore printed as soon as possible and appeared throughout the town. "The Mission Committee earnestly request the prayers of all Christian people for God's blessing on the special effort now being made to spread the knowledge of Christ in this town "

In the evening there were either services in the churches or in the school-rooms of those parishes taking part in the Mission, generally in the school-rooms, when an opportunity was afforded to the incumbents to introduce the Missioners, and together with them to address some words of counsel to the people In many cases the Saturday evening meeting was for communicants and church workers only, when final arrangements were made, and the Missioner pointed out to the latter the way in which he desired them to render assistance during the coming week. The Mission properly commenced on Sunday, January 24th, though the first note had been already struck, for on the previous Thursday, the 21st, addresses were given in the Civil Court, Town Hall, to the policemen on day duty, and on Friday, the 22nd, to those on night duty, by the Rev. E T Leeke, of Cambridge, and the Rev. T W Swift, of Everton, Liverpool.

The following is a list of the churches, together with the names of the Incumbents and the Missioners taking part in the work.

The movement was almost universal. Certainly never in the history of the Church in Leeds had there been witnessed such united action as in the arrangements for, and in the carrying out of the Mission

Church.	Incumbent.	Mission Preachers.
Parish Church ...	. Rev. Dr. Gott	. Rev G. H. Wilkinson, St Peter's, Eaton Square, London; Rev. James Moore, Whatley; and Rev. George A. Robins, Bishopstone
Holy Trinity .	Rev J H. McCheane	Rev. E. Snowden, Huddersfield.

Church	Incumbent.	Mission Preachers.
Armley Hall	Rev J Maughan	Rev W. A Scott, New Seaham.
Christ Church	Rev J G. Smith	Rev W. H. Lowder, Manchester, and Rev J. S. Tute, Markington.
Christ Ch., Upper Armley	Rev. J Thompson	Rev G K. Flindt, St. Matthew's, Denmark Hill, London
St Saviour	Rev R Collins	Rev. R. Linklater, St. Peter's, London Docks, and Rev C. I. Black, Burley-in-Wharfedale.
All Saints	Rev. P S. Duval	Rev H A D Surridge, London.
St Alban	Rev J. T. Maguinness	Rev. N. F. N'Neile, Ripon
St. Andrew	Rev. B. Mills	Rev. Canon Hitchcock, Whitburn
St Bartholomew, Armley	Rev. F. G H Smith	Rev. F G H. Smith
St Clement	Rev T S Fleming	Rev. G J Watts, Sheffield
St Edmund	Rev E W. Makinson	Rev W B Brown, East Shefford.
St George	Rev S Adams	Rev. Prebendary Macdonald, Kersal, and Rev. J W. K. Disney, Clareborough.
St Hilda	Rev W J Scarlin	Rev T R Willacy, Fallowfield
St. James	Rev E Jackson	Rev. W H M H Aitken, Everton
St. John	Rev H Temple	Rev Canon Wilde, Louth, and Rev R Bullock, Barrow-on-Humber.
St. John, New Wortley.	Rev. S. P. Lampen	Rev. B Cassin, Bolton; and Rev S E Pennefather, Wakefield
St John, Newtown	Rev J. Hepher	Rev. A. Williamson, St. Peter's, Eaton Square, London, and Rev J E Brown, Holmer.
St. Jude, Hunslet	Rev. J H Goodier	Rev G Everard, Wolverhampton
St Luke, Beeston Hill	Rev J. Lobley	Rev. J. Lobley

Church.	Incumbent.	Mission Preachers.
St Luke	Rev C H D. Williams	Rev. H Baxter, Shipton; and Rev. C. S Towle, Moordown.
St Mary	Rev J Bickerdike	. Rev W. Dunkerley, Yoxall; Rev J H Lester, Derby, and Rev. H Martin, Sunderland.
St Matthew .	Rev. Dr. Flood	Rev H. Fawcett, Stepney, and Rev. F L. Allen, Chilcombe
St Matthew, Holbeck	Rev J H F. Kendall	. Rev J H F. Kendall
Chapeltown	Rev. R. R Kirby	.. Rev C. Green, Bishopwearmouth.
Burley	Rev F L Harrison	Rev.W Milton, Sheffield.
Buslingthorpe .	Rev F M Theed	Rev. T W Swift, Everton, and Rev. J. W Diggle, Walton
St Paul	Rev J R Stratten	Rev E. T. Leeke, Cambridge, and Rev. J. J. Scott, Cambridge
St Peter, Hunslet Moor.	Rev. J. H. Evans	. Rev. J. H. Evans.
Bramley ..	... Rev S. W Cope	Rev F Barker, Middleham.
St. Philip ..	Rev J M Fawcett	. Rev. J. C Hordern, Kirby Grindalyth, and Rev Newton Mant, Plympton St Mary
St Silas, Hunslet	Rev. A C. Downer	Rev W Hayton, New Shildon; and Rev. J.B. Cane, Weston.
St Simon .	Rev. Thos Whitby	Rev W. T. Storrs, Heckmondwike, and Rev. T. Storrs, Hull
Burmantofts .	... Rev. A H Kelk	Rev H Sharpe, Hampstead; and Rev W H. Brigg, Bolton.
Stanningley .	Rev C F Booker	.. Rev. G. L. Kemp, Oxford.
Farnley Ironworks	.. Rev H J Geer	Rev J. Ellison, Sowerby Bridge; and Rev. F. Courtney, Glasgow
Borough Gaol ...	... Rev. O Cookson	. Rev. A. C Smith, Middlesborough.

It would obviously be impossible to give many particulars of each day's proceedings as the Mission advanced, to recount

the modes employed in the various parishes to further the
objects of the Mission, or to enter into details by describing the
services of every church. In some respects all the churches
were alike, and in others each differed from the rest. The
arrangements in the various parishes were made by the
Parochial Clergy and the Missioner of the parish. It must
suffice to give a general outline of the proceedings, but for the
sake of definiteness, and on other grounds which will commend
themselves to all, a more extended account will be furnished of
the work as carried on at the Leeds Parish Church.

In all the churches the seats were free throughout the week.

In many the daily services began with the Holy Communion,
or Morning Prayer, with a short address by Mission Preacher,
at hours varying in different districts from 5 a m. to 10 a m.

In the course of the morning, Prayers and Address. Between
12 and 1, in some of the manufacturing districts of the town,
a short service was held, consisting of Hymn, Prayer, and
Address, which working people were invited to attend on the
way to or from dinner in their working dress A Scripture
Reader or Church Worker frequently stood at the door of a
large mill, to tell the workpeople as they left the mill of the
service, and either by a handbill or by word of mouth to urge
them to come to it.

In the afternoon special classes were invited to the church.
" Wives and Mothers ," " Women only ;" "Servants ," " Day
and Sunday Scholars," &c

Then came the evening service, with that which is com-
monly regarded as distinguishing a Mission from Special
Services, viz.—an After-meeting

Almost in every instance the After-meeting was held in the
Church itself

There was much diversity in the manner of conducting it.

In some cases, at the conclusion of the service and sermon,
the Missioner invited the whole congregation to remain, and
the Meeting consisted of Hymns, Addresses, reading por-
tions of Holy Scripture, and extemporary Prayer.

In others, the Mission Preacher asked those only to remain for the After-meeting who were anxious about their souls and desired spiritual counsel and guidance.

Or, again, believers in Christ were requested to remain with inquirers after salvation, that united prayers for pardon and peace might be offered on behalf of those whom the Holy Spirit had brought to repentance.

In most cases, whilst the Scriptures were read and Prayers offered, the Missioner moved silently about the church, and spoke with those who wished for instruction in the things of God, and who had not yet been able to realise a present Saviour and to enjoy peace in believing, or who longed to know the way of God more perfectly

On many of the parochial bills announcing the time of services during the week, persons desirous of consulting the Mission Preacher were invited to do so, either in the parsonage or the vestry, at specified hours

In most of the churches there was a special service for men only, generally in the afternoon of either the first or second Sunday of the Mission.

The Bible Society having made a grant of 10,000 or 11,000 copies of single Gospels, they were in many churches given to the men at the close of these services.

Church Workers, both male and female, were largely employed in visiting persons, in the districts assigned to them, half an hour or an hour before the evening Services, and inviting them to come to the House of God; some made it their business to try and induce the loiterers at street corners, at the doors, or even within the doors of public houses, to come In a few parishes bands of earnest workers marched down the street singing, the procession increasing as it advanced, and usually the march ended only when the often motley assembly arrived within the church at the time, carefully arranged, when Divine Service was about to commence. Sometimes short, heart-stirring, and pointed addresses were given at intervals on the route

C

Leeds Parish Church.—Long before the Mission began the clergy connected with the Parish Church met regularly for special prayer and preparation; meetings, too, of the Church workers and communicants were held weekly for a time, and afterwards twice a week, in the Church, for the same object

Thousands of tracts and papers, many of them written by the Rev. G H. Wilkinson, the chief Parish Church Missioner, were distributed.

As many as twenty-eight clergymen took part in the work of the Mission in connection with this Church

The Mission was inaugurated on Saturday afternoon, January 23rd, when the Rev. G. H. Wilkinson addressed about 150 of the district visitors and other Church workers   The services during the ten days were as follows —Sundays—7 45, Short Meditation ; 8, Holy Communion ; 10 30, Morning Prayer, Litany, Sermon, and Holy Communion , 2 15, Children's Service and Address , 3 30, Special Address to Men ; 6 30, Evening Prayer, Sermon, and After-meeting. Week days—7 30, Holy Communion, with Short Meditation ; 9 15, Address to School Children ; 10, Morning Prayer and Holy Communion ; 11 15, Mission Address , 12, Service for Church Workers, with Special Prayer ; 4, Evening Prayer , 7 30, Mission Service and After-meeting   There were, on an average, 100 communicants every day at the two celebrations —at the earlier of which a meditation of a practical or devotional character was given by the Rev G A. Robins, and the numbers who came to listen to the address at a quarter-past eleven became larger and larger every day   At night there was always a vast congregation at the Special Mission Service, a great majority remaining for the After-meeting, while on the two week-day evenings many were unable to find room in the Church.   The subjects of the evening Addresses by Mr. Wilkinson were—1 The Sending of the Messenger   2 Sin 3. Decision. 4 The Atonement   5 Implicit Trust.   6. The Life of Faith.   7. The Tenderness of Christ   8 Holy Joy The special services for men were largely attended, particularly

on the second Sunday, when there must have been at least
2,000 men present, who listened for nearly an hour and a half
with rapt attention to the burning words spoken by the chief
Missioner On the same Sunday evening nearly as many must
have been sent away as those who were in the Church, which
was more than crowded in every corner. On the Tuesday
evening there was a special thanksgiving service, to which all
were invited who had received any blessing from God during
the Mission The memorial cards were given away at a special
service on the Wednesday evening This also was a very
solemn and touching occasion, which will not soon be forgotten
by those who were present. In addition to the regular
services, there were three meetings daily during the
Mission week for the women who attend the different mothers'
meetings in the parish, two meetings for men on the Saturday
afternoon, a daily meeting in the Mill Street School room,
specially intended for those employed at Messrs Holdforth's
silk mill, and service on the Sunday evenings in the Mission
School room in St. Peter's Square Nearly 1,000 children
were present at the services intended for them on week-
days and Sundays, and frequent addresses were given to special
classes, such as the day school teachers, the members of the
guilds, communicants' classes, and the like A meeting for
prayer amongst Church workers was held daily at noon under
the direction of the Rev J H. Moore, who gave a short address
at the beginning of each meeting A great number of persons
availed themselves of this opportunity of joining in united
intercession for God's blessing upon the Mission; and there
can be no doubt that these prayers were a great help`and
encouragement to those who were engaged in the work At
the After-meetings the Church was divided into twenty-five
blocks, and as many clergymen, together with laymen and
experienced Christian women, spoke with those who desired
counsel and comfort

That which has been said respecting the crowded state of
the Parish Church might be said almost equally of several

Churches of the town   Concern for the soul, the wish to hear
of Christ and the way of salvation, was not confined to any
one parish or district   Churches on every side were filled to
overflowing, so much so that services were held in many
Schools for those who were unable to obtain admittance in
the Churches.

An interesting but very unusual service should not pass
unrecorded here   One Sunday afternoon the Rev. Edward
Jackson delivered a Special Address (which was interpreted
by Mr. Foulston, Superintendent of the Deaf and Dumb
Institution) to the deaf and dumb of Leeds, in St James's
Church.

So far the Churches.   Much might be said of the most
interesting gatherings in the workshops, where thousands in
the place where they earned the bread that perisheth, heard of
that Divine Bread which gives life to the world.

The following is a list of the Bishop's engagements during
the week :—

Monday, Jan 25th.—At Messrs Greenwood and Batley's;
and Messrs. Manning, Wardle and Co.'s

Tuesday, 26th —At Messrs Fowler and Co.'s; and to the
miners, in the Miners' Institute, York Road

Wednesday, 27th —At Farnley Ironworks , Messrs Kitson
and Co.'s , and Messrs Tetley and Sons.

Thursday, 28th —At Messrs. Taylor Brothers and Co 's ,
and Kirkstall Forge Company.

Friday, 29th —At Messrs. Lawson and Sons'; and Messrs.
Whitham and Sons'

Saturday, 30th.—At Messrs Cooper and Co 's, Hunslet.

No one who was present at any of these services can forget
the unwonted spectacle   A waggon or engine, sometimes
formed the pulpit   Huge pieces of machinery, destined
for different parts of the world, surrounded, or were visible
amongst, the crowd of hearers ; men and boys were often seen
perched in most apparently impossible places, on beams,
cranes, and steam-hammers

It had been thought by some persons that slight disturbances would take place at the meetings, caused not through a spirit of opposition or malice, but arising out of mere thoughtlessness and frivolity, yet nothing of the kind ever appeared, on "the sea of upturned faces" earnestness and devoutness were evident. The services were of the most solemn and impressive character

A paper containing the four well-known Hymns, "Jesu, Lover of my Soul," "Just as I am," "Rock of Ages," and "When I survey the wondrous Cross," was given to each man, and the singing of the hymns was most hearty.

Similar gatherings were held throughout the Borough in mills, large shops, tanneries, cap manufactories, in short to almost every trade and business carried on in this town, remarkable probably above all towns in the variety of its manufactures, the Gospel Message was taken   Sometimes the parochial Clergy, sometimes the Missioners of the Parish gave the addresses, occasionally both.

In one parish certainly, where many mills, large and small, are situated, probably in others too, not a single mill but had its religious service and addresses during the week.   At the workshops for the Blind (in St. John's parish), the Rev. Henry Temple, Vicar, and the Rev. Canon Wilde, Missioner of St. John's, gave addresses.

A wonderful instance of the deep interest felt in these gatherings by the workpeople themselves may be given.

In one of the poorest parts of the East end of Leeds is a large Mill, in which more than 2000 persons, chiefly girls, a large proportion of them Roman Catholics, are employed. The owner of the mill, a Churchman, and personally favourable to the Mission, thought it would be most unadvisable to invite or allow a Missioner to address his employés. When early in the week he learned that an open air meeting was to be held near his premises, he wrote to the Vicar of the parish and to the Rural Dean expostulating, declaring that there would be a riot; that it would be most imprudent in a neigh-

bourhood where so many were Roman Catholics, and so many
utterly Godless, to attempt to give an address

Later in the week, however, the same gentleman wrote
again, requesting that a service might be held in his mill, as
he had learned that there was great dissatisfaction felt and
expressed by his employés that they had had no opportunity
like those working in the factories around of hearing an
address   Roman Catholics and Protestants were alike anxious
for a service   It need scarcely be added, that the service was
held, and those present forming a vast crowd, joined heartily in it.

Numerous instances might be given in which the workpeople
requested the Mission Preacher or Incumbent of a parish to
come and address them, the meeting being held in their own
and not in the master's time.

As it was found that the large class of men employed by the
Railway Companies, porters, guards, &c, chiefly lived in New
Wortley and Armley Hall parishes, a service was held specially for these men at the former church in the afternoon of
Sunday, January 24th, when the Rev S Pennefather preached,
and on January 31st, at the latter church, sermon by the Bishop
of Ripon ; the churches were crowded, and hundreds of
persons were unable to obtain admittance

The hotel servants at the Great Northern and Queen Hotels
having expressed the wish to have a service, the Rev. J. H.
Moore spent an evening at each of those places, and conducted
the services.

Post office and telegraph employés were addressed in the
Instrument Room at the Post Office, on the second Sunday of
the Mission, by the Rev. H. Stewart   About 300 postmen,
sorters of letters, males and females employed in sending and
receiving telegraph messages, and boys employed in carrying
them out, attended and filled the room.   During the meeting
the familiar click of the needle was heard at one or other of
the instruments, and a clerk quietly left his place to record the
tidings.   Not unfrequently it was found that the message was
sent from Birmingham and other towns, expressing interest

in the meeting for postal and telegraphic officials, which the sender knew was taking place in Leeds at that moment.

A special Mission was organised to the unhappy class of fallen women. A house was taken as a temporary home for any who desired to leave their evil courses, and a lady appointed to manage it. Several ladies undertook to go out, two and two, and visit daily the houses in which the women lived, in order to try and turn them from the error of their ways. This truly Christian effort has not been without success. Several have been (in some cases after remaining a few days in the temporary home) sent to permanent refuges.

The Mission took the Borough Gaol within the field of its operations. The Rev. A. C. Smith, Middlesborough, conducted the work there. It need scarcely be said that a Mission in a prison is a very rare if not an altogether unique event.

Daily Special Services were held in the Guardian Asylum, and were conducted by the Rev. J. W. K. Disney, Missioner at St George's (in which parish the Asylum is situated). Addresses were given in the Working Men's Hall by the Rev. Prebendary Macdonald, also St. George's Missioner.

As the Mission Committee were advised by gentlemen (chiefly members of the Society of Friends), who had for years taken a practical interest in the temporal and spiritual welfare of cabmen and tram conductors, that it would be best to postpone any special work amongst that class until Lent, when fewer cabs would be employed, and the men more free to attend meetings, on February 15th and February 16th, about four hundred cabmen, tram conductors and drivers, and their wives, were entertained at supper in the Friends' Meeting House, Woodhouse Lane. The expense was borne in part by the gentlemen before referred to, and in part by the Mission fund. Addresses were given on the first night by the Rev. S. Adams, Mr Thomas Harvey, Mr S. Southall, and the Rev. T. W Swift, of Everton; and, on the second, by the Rev Dr Gott and the Rev J. W Diggle, of Walton.

Each day during the Mission week a public meeting for prayer, with addresses by two Missioners, was held from 2.15

to 3.0 p.m , in the Hall of the Church Institute, and was largely attended   When not prevented by other engagements the Bishop presided.

The following took part in conducting the meetings —

Monday, Jan 25th . ..	Rev G. EVERARD, Wolverhampton
	Rev. W. T STORRS, Heckmondwike.
Tuesday, Jan. 26th .	. Rev. C. GREEN, Bishop Wearmouth
	Rev Canon WILDE, Louth.
Wednesday, Jan. 27th	Rev J H MOORE, Whatley
'	Rev W. A SCOTT, New Seaham
Thursday, Jan. 28th	Rev E. T LEEKE, Cambridge.
	Rev. T. W SWIFT, Everton
Friday, Jan 29th .	Rev F. E ALLEN, Chilcombe.
	Rev W. MILTON, Sheffield
Saturday, Jan 30th .	Rev. F PIGOU, Doncaster
	Rev E. SNOWDEN, Huddersfield

Though not directly connected with, or arranged by, the Mission Committee, any description of the Leeds Mission which omitted reference to the daily meetings conducted by the Rev W. H M. H Aitken, of Everton, Liverpool, Missioner at St. James's, Leeds, would be most incomplete, both on account of the numbers who attended them, and the signal blessing that rested upon them.

Mr. Aitken gave his heart-stirring appeals, January 25th to 28th, from 12 to 1, in the Young Men's Christian Association Hall, and on the 29th, 30th, and Feb 1st, in the Albert Hall , but hundreds not being able to enter, the Victoria (Town) Hall was taken, and even that building, though it accommodated 4,000 persons, proved far too small for the requirements The Town Hall Services were brought to a conclusion by a Prayer Meeting, held on Saturday night, Feb 6th

But now, having given some, though necessarily an incomplete, account of the Origin and History of the Leeds Mission, it remains to ask—What has been the Result? There were long and anxious preparations for it ; thought and care and toil were expended ; prayers were offered in family circles, in churches, in school-rooms, in sick chambers, in private and in public—not only in Leeds, but in distant places

It was known here, that during the Mission Week petitions were publicly offered to God in at least sixty churches in different parts of the world; in Cornwall and other English counties, in Scotland, in Ireland, in France, in India

Missioners came from busy towns and quiet country parishes, Church Workers of every rank toiled and prayed, crowded meetings and crowded churches were seen on every hand; men who for years had never been within the doors of a House of God, and who at first seemed utterly at a loss what to do when there or how to follow the service, were found night after night listening to the Gospel Message It has been computed that during the Mission about 40,000 persons were at one and the same time listening to the Word of God. But what is the outcome of the whole? Has the Mission been like a flash in the pan, a temporary excitement, a nine days' wonder?

What is the produce of the vast machinery set in motion? With so much sowing of the good seed, is there any fruit?

To begin with, so manifestly had the Divine presence and blessing been felt during the Mission Week, that the clergy, unknown to each other, announced that in their various churches, a Special Service of Thanksgiving would be held And there was a universal feeling amongst the Missioners, Parochial Clergy, and Church Workers, that there should be, for themselves specially, a United Service of Praise to God for His goodness to them, and for prospering their work.

This last took place on Monday morning, Feb. 1st, in the Parish Church It consisted of the Administration of the Holy Communion, and Sermon by the Bishop of Ripon, from Rev i. 5, 6· "Unto Him that loved us, and washed us from our sins in His own blood, and hath made us kings and priests unto God and His Father; to Him be glory and dominion for ever and ever. Amen."   The Bishop said· "We meet together in this sacred place to offer up our united praises and thanksgiving to God for the blessing which He has been pleased to pour down upon the Mission. I believe very few of us fully anticipated so copious a shower of blessing as that which has been received. God has abundantly answered our

prayers He has been better to us than our fears Far be it
from me to use the language of exaggeration, but I think on
reviewing what has taken place during the last week, I am not
mistaken in saying that this large and important community
has been deeply stirred. There has been a remarkable
unanimity amongst the clergy with respect to this great work
With very few exceptions the whole body of the clergy of
Leeds have thrown themselves into it ; and I learn with the
deepest satisfaction, that through all the preparatory work
that has been going on for months with respect to it, there has
not been one jarring note of discord: all has been harmony;
all have been of one mind.

"The Mission has been remarkably characterised by the
absence of every kind of excess and of undue excitement.
There has been a very kind and generous feeling expressed on
behalf of the Mission by all classes of the community. Even
those who do not belong to our own Church have, neverthe-
less, wished God-speed to the effort; and, if I am rightly
informed, in the chapels of some of our Nonconforming
brethren, prayers have been offered that God would pour down
His abundant grace upon this great effort to win souls to
Christ. Most of the principal firms in Leeds have kindly
thrown open their places of work to allow the preaching of the
everlasting Gospel to the hands whom they employ. Those
opportunities were freely accepted by the men for whose
benefit they were intended Our churches have been crowded
with eager and attentive listeners Many have come inquiring
about their soul's salvation. Many have been anxious who
were never anxious before about their spiritual state, and can
we for a moment doubt that many, through God's grace, have
been brought to Jesus, and have found joy and peace in believing, and that a fresh anthem of praise has resounded through
the courts of heaven over many a returning sinner brought to
God, instrumentally through this Mission ? . . . . On the
review of the Mission, the first feeling which ought to be
uppermost in our minds is one of profound humility. All the
uccess of a Mission like this is of God, and not of man. It is

not man's eloquence, nor man's imagination, nor any gifts
which God may have granted to any to possess, but if there is
any success, as we doubt not there has been, 'Not unto us, O
Lord, not unto us, but unto thy Name give the praise'   The
next feeling we ought to cherish is one of greater personal
devotedness to our blessed Lord and Master   Every one who
takes any part in Missions ought to look for an increase of
spiritual grace in his own soul   We should also, on reviewing
the Mission, cherish a feeling of greater earnestness than ever
in seeking the salvation of souls around us   Let us bind ourselves on this, the day of our thanksgiving, that we will with
redoubled energy devote ourselves to the work of trying to
bring poor wandering sinners to the feet of Christ"

The service closed most appropriately with singing the
Te Deum

It is perhaps premature at this early period to speak much
of the results of the Mission.   Our judgment is often at fault
when we try to estimate the spiritual effect produced by either
the ordinary or extraordinary means employed to advance
Christ's kingdom   Only at the Great Day shall we know truly
and fully what have been the real and abiding results of the
Mission, it will then doubtless be seen that some of the good
seed scattered so widely during the Mission, and which we in
our ignorance hoped and believed fell on the good ground and
was destined to bring forth fruit to God's glory, only after all
fell on stony places and among thorns, and it will also be seen
that blessings were brought to many of whom in this world
the Missioner will never hear, that the seed which to human
appearance had only fallen by the way-side, was yet to bring
forth much fruit.

Amongst the results of the Mission may be mentioned the
following :—

1. Large additions to the congregations in the churches
throughout the town.   Many persons who have long neglected
public worship now esteem it a duty and a privilege to "come
into His presence with thanksgiving"   The increase in the
attendance at church on Good Friday (March 26th), and the

more general observance of that solemn day were very evident.

2. Many who lived in sin, regardless of the offers of mercy or of God's claims upon them, have, so far as man can judge, been brought to a saving knowledge of Christ. Christianity, which to numbers was nothing more than a name, has become to them a reality. The marks of spiritual life are seen where before there was only a form of godliness. Bible Classes, and Communicants' Classes, have been commenced, or, where they before existed, have received additional members.

Memorial cards were printed at the close of the Mission for those who desired to possess them, with these words :—

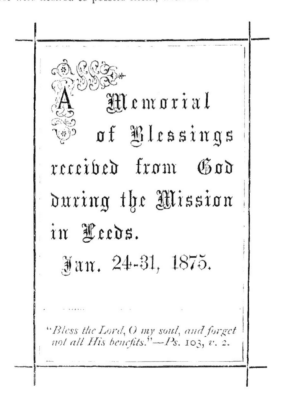

A Memorial of Blessings received from God during the Mission in Leeds.

Jan. 24-31, 1875.

"Bless the Lord, O my soul, and forget not all His benefits."—Ps. 103, v. 2.

Some thousands of persons applied to the clergy for them, and received them.

3. At the Confirmation, held in Leeds a few weeks after the Mission, 2,030 persons, an unusual proportion of whom were adults, in that solemn ordinance declared themselves to be Christ's servants The increase in the number of candidates will be seen when compared with the average of past years—1,200 to 1,400—the number last year was 1,314.

4. A greater desire for and striving after holiness in the people of God, a longing to run the way of God's commandments.

Many who have long professed to love Christ, but have hitherto done little to advance His Kingdom, are now asking the question, "Lord, what wilt Thou have me to do?" And they are entering various fields of usefulness. District visitors, tract distributors, Sunday School teachers, and other Church workers have vastly increased in numbers as a direct result of the Mission

5 Greater confidence in God and trust in His promises, and a deeper sense of the power of prayer are felt by Christians generally.

Whilst external testimonies to the truth of the written Word are being multiplied by the researches in Moab, in Palestine, in Assyria, the events of the Mission show that the Word of God, mighty in the early days of the Church, has lost none of its power, by the Holy Spirit's blessing, to subdue the rebellious will, to soften the hard heart, that the Gospel is as ever "the power of God unto salvation to every one that believeth"

6. A more kindly spirit has pervaded the various Christian denominations towards each other.

The *Leeds Mercury*, of January 25th, stated that on the previous day (the first Sunday of the Mission) "In most of the Nonconformist chapels of the town, reference was made to the Mission, and cordial wishes expressed for its success In some cases sermons bearing upon the movement were preached, and the members of various congregations were advised to attend as many as possible of the special services during the week." And the counsel was widely followed

The *Mercury* of February 2nd, mentioned the fact that the minister of one of the leading Congregational Chapels in the town preached on the second Sunday of the Mission to a large congregation, on "The Results of the Mission." Having spoken of the aim of the Mission—to reach all classes—the preparation in every parish by prayer meetings, tract distribution, &c, the organization of the Mission, the unsectarian tone of the addresses, and, above all, of its spiritual results, he added that the Mission illustrated his text ("there shall be showers of blessing"). Like the showers, it was from above; it was copious, impartial, seasonable, refreshing, life-giving in its influences, and quiet in its processes

The following correspondence, which appeared in the Leeds newspapers, will show the good feeling that existed, and was expressed at the close of the Mission between the clergy and Nonconformists.

"THE RECENT MISSION IN LEEDS

" We have been requested to publish the following correspondence —

" The Vicarage, Leeds, Feby 16th, 1875.

" My dear Mr. Jowitt,

" I very gladly send you a copy of a resolution of the Leeds Chapter, which we passed in our meeting yesterday

" It expresses both my own feelings and those of the Leeds clergy generally, and I shall be glad if you will convey it to those whom it concerns in any way that seems most proper to yourself.

" I am, my dear Mr. Jowitt, yours very sincerely,

(Signed)   'JOHN GOTT,

" John Jowitt, Esq. '   "Rural Dean of Leeds

" Resolution passed in the Leeds Chapter of Clergy."

February, 15th, 1875.

That the deepfelt and hearty thanks of the clergy of the Rural Deanery of Leeds be given to the ministers, employers of labour, and others in the several Nonconformist bodies of the borough, for their prayers and the sympathy which they have given to the Church of England during the mission week; and they pray to God to render them an hundredfold for this their Christian feeling.

(Signed)   JOHN GOTT,
Rural Dean of Leeds.

"My dear Dr. Gott,   "Leeds, Feb. 17, 1875

"I am much obliged by your kind note of the 16th inst., inclosing the resolution of the Leeds Chapter, held on the previous day.

"Availing myself of the permission given, I am sending your letter and the resolution to the newspapers.

"Most heartily congratulating you on the great blessing which has attended the Mission—a blessing happily felt by very many outside of the Established Church.

"I am, dear Dr. Gott,
"Yours faithfully,
"JOHN JOWITT.
"The Rev. John Gott, D D , Rural Dean of Leeds."

7. The Clergy of the town have much to thank God for, as they see and experience the effects of the Mission

A greater spirit of brotherly union has been awakened amongst them. They have witnessed tokens of God's presence in their several Churches: they are encouraged to labour on with greater zeal and hopefulness, knowing that He who has sent, in such rich abundance, the supplies of grace during the past Mission, will not withhold them in their future work.

Several of the Clergy, who at first consented to take part in the Mission, did so with some degree of misgiving, hesitation, and doubt as to the usefulness of the contemplated movement. Reports had reached them of extravagances and eccentricities that had marked the proceedings elsewhere, and they feared lest these which, after all, had been but the accidents of some, might be in the nature of all Missions.

Now, however, most assuredly, there is not a single Clergyman who took any part, even the humblest, in the Leeds Mission, but is right thankful to God that he did not stand aloof, but was enabled to take his share in the blessed work, and that he came to the help of the Lord against the mighty; not one but will now go forth to labour for his Master with greater trust and joy in God, and a deeper sense of his responsibility to, and of the nearness of Him, who is the Chief Shepherd, and who has given him his commission to call sinners to repentance, and to feed the flock of God.

On every ground then, as we look back on the solemn time of refreshing from the presence of God, vouchsafed during and since the Mission, Christians generally, Ministers and people alike, whatever of difficulty or opposition may betide in the future, have abundant reason to thank God and take courage.

Lightning Source UK Ltd.
Milton Keynes UK
UKHW020919150822
407319UK00007B/1459

CPSIA information can be obtained at www.ICGtesting.com
Printed in the USA
LVOW01s2054290514

387793LV00030B/1119/P

9 781611 452099